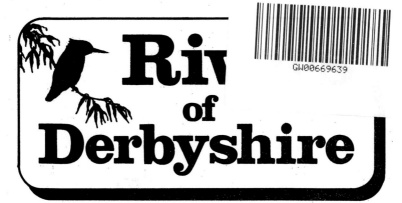

Rivers of Derbyshire

Harold W. Fearnehough

original illustrations by Caroline Abrahams

© 1990

ISBN 0 946404 27 5

WALK & WRITE LTD.,
UNIT 1, MOLYNEUX BUSINESS PARK,
WHITWORTH ROAD, DARLEY DALE,
MATLCOK, DERBYSHIRE. DE4 2HJ

TEL/FAX - 01629 - 735911

THE DERBYSHIRE HERITAGE SERIES

The Derbyshire Heritage Series -

The chief joy of the Peak District
is its rivers,
and it is doubtful
if any other region can show
such a group
of
glorious streams.

J.H. Ingram

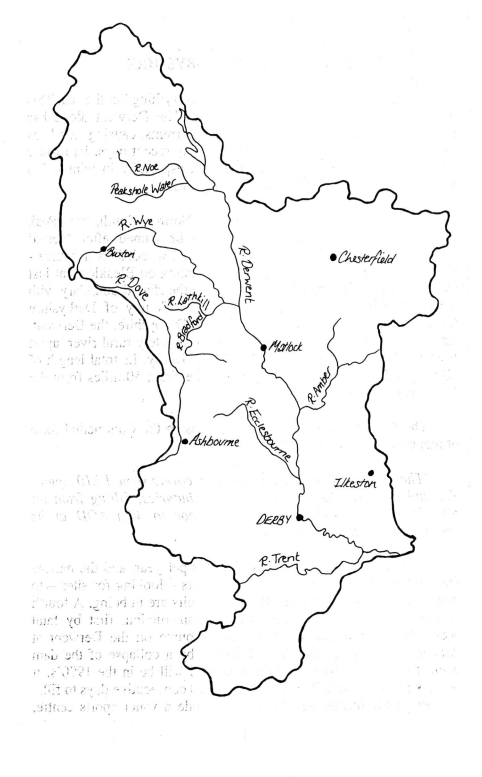

THE RIVERS OF DERBYSHIRE

It has been said that Derbyshire has everything but the sea. This does not mean that it is short of water. The Derwent alone has constantly been hurling down its surplus torrents, causing floods as far south as the County Town even in fairly recent days. Its former undammed forces can only be imagined, especially in winter. No wonder Defoe described it as a 'fury of a river.'

Derbyshire rivers flow roughly from North to South, from Peak to Lowlands. The Derwent, thought to be named after 'derva' meaning 'oaks' - indicative of a former well wooded river course - rises on 'lofty, pathless moorlands culminating on Bleaklow' at just over 2,000 feet. It forms for a short while the shared boundary with Yorkshire, bisecting a little unequally the County of Derbyshire from North to South. Though dominant in Derbyshire, the Derwent, from its source at Swain's Greave, is a completely rural river, apart from its short passage through the City of Derby. Its total length of 60 miles takes it to its confluence with the Trent 50 miles from the North Sea.

The Severn Trent Water Authority, using the Continental form of mensuration, states:-

'The catchment of the River Derwent covers some 1,210 square Km and the river itself excluding its tributaries, falling from an altitude of 630m AOD on Howden Moor to 30m AOD at its confluence with the River Trent.'

A heavy rainfall of around 60 inches per year, and the narrow Derwent Valley, influenced water engineers – looking for sites – to build impounding reservoirs. Three reservoirs are in being. A fourth at Carsington has been delayed in its construction, first by fatal accidents in tunnelling from the water source on the Derwent at Ambergate pumping station, and further by a collapse of the dam wall. It is now expected that the water fill will be in the 1990's. It will take 50 million gallons per day for 150 consecutive days to fill.

Plans for further developments include a water sports centre, with boat slipways on 44 acres of land overlooking the reservoir. It is also hoped to include a leisure park with a nature trail, together with a restaurant and a hotel, with landscaped car parking areas.

Howden Reservoir was the first to be built (1901-12), Derwent followed (1902-16) and Ladybower, after nationwide opposition, was begun in 1935. It is the largest in the British Isles, having an earthwork embankment, and covers 50 acres. It has a capacity of 6,300,000,000 gallons. The need for water outweighed the demand for resources of materials and manpower even in wartime, and work continued during World War Two. Filling with water commenced in 1943 and included an extra 7 million gallons, already diverted from the Ashop and Alport, into the Derwent Reservoir. Ladybower Reservoir was opened officially by King George VI on September 25th. 1945. It had replaced four other reservoirs previously planned, brought together the Corporations of Derby, Nottingham, Sheffield and Leicester, albeit a little uneasily at first, and the Severn Trent Water Authority was set up to replace the Derwent Valley Water Board of 1899.

Ladybower Reservoir

Beautiful valleys and the historic villages of Derwent and Ashopton were lost. Left behind was 'the silent valley' deprived of Derwent Hall and Church. There were the difficulties and needs of exhumation and reburial at Bamford Church and all that entailed in local objection and ancient civil and church law. A story in itself, it tended to become accepted, though not likely to be forgotten by a tale unforgettably told, in immense detail, by Dr. Brian Robinson. In his book "Birchinlee", he gave the name to the purpose-built village of 'Tin Town' as it was colloquially known, whose corrugated roofs sheltered the homes of the men who built the early dams, the women who supported them, the tradesmen who supplied their needs, the teachers who taught their children, the doctor and nurses who cared for them in ill-health and after frequent injury, and the preachers who looked after their spiritual needs. All told, Birchinlee had 1,000 inhabitants. Some of its personnel, and even its railway lines, saw service in the 1914-18 war.

The Severn Trent Authority pressed on with its statutory duties and few were left to remember the Derwent as 'little more than a babbling brook.' The necessity for collection and treatment of water grew apace, not merely to meet human needs, but also increasing industrial use. Meanwhile the call for conservation grew.

Benefits have accrued to many, in that water-borne sports and similar activities have become both possible and permitted, subject to stringent anti-pollution regulations. Provision is also made for anglers, probably the most prolific and responsible users of inland waters, though there are those who rail about the effect on birds of carelessly discarded lead weights and wires. However, the Severn Trent Water Authority seems satisfied with those who fish to the extent that it provides special car parking facilities at Ladybower.

An establishment alongside the reservoir breeds Rainbow, Brown and Brook Trout for re-stocking the reservoir, and issues tickets for fishing. On the reservoir wall a plaque denotes a fishing stage for the disabled sponsored by the Severn Trent Water Authority and the Hope Valley Lions. It was officially opened by the Duke of Devonshire on 23rd. March 1984.

7

From Ladybower, the Derwent looks no more than 'a ribbon of water with a little waterfall' by the two-arched Yorkshire Bridge, so called as the last major crossing before the road moves on into that county. The crossings of the Derwent range from clapper to motorway bridges with a fine range of old stone bridges in between. For years they had served the jaggers, carrying panniered goods on horse-back, at river crossings, before they returned to safer and more direct ways over the hills. From its source, the Derwent never leaves the roadway for more than a mile; roadmakers could not improve on the river's unerring penetration of the terrain, the route also followed by the railways. Bridges replaced earlier fords, for example at Bamford, Hazelford, Grindleford, Cromford and Milford, originally Muleford.

At Mytholm Bridge, the Noe joins the Derwent, fresh from Roman Anavio, now Brough. There are stepping stones as the Derwent widens, part of an old track from Sheffield. Beyond the Church at Hope, the Noe has picked up Peakshole Water from the darknesses of Peak Cavern, shorn of its Anglo-Saxon title, presumably to appease Victorian ears.

Flowing on between Win Hill and Lose Hill, said to be the choice of victor and defeated in a very early battle, the river is soon augmented by waters from Crowden and Grinds Brooks and Jaggers Clough, the latter a nominal relic of men with four-legged beasts of burden.

From Mytham Bridge to Hathersage, 'the scenery is of a pastoral and peaceful character,' writes Leyland. The many visitors and the many commutors living in the environs of Derwent can scarcely be aware of the change that has taken place, for now it is difficult to realise that much of the spectacular scenery of the former Derwent Estates and Hope woodlands is less than a hundred years old, a man made by-product of the building of the three reservoirs.

Hathersage occupies 'a fine position' a mile and a half downstream from the bridge, with an old ford and a former leadmill with only age rounded spoilheaps and derelict engine houses remaining. Hazelford Bridge, one mile to the south, has long been known as 'Leadmill Bridge', recalling early industry which, as in many areas of Derbyshire, had some farming as an adjunct to provide subsistence when mining was impossible. Such circumstances were indicated in the vernacular by a miner who said, "Eh, lad, they could but nobbut work one day i' fower, they were licked to't'world wi watter.'

Changing and advancing industry at Hathersage took metal from the ground and water from the river to produce tools, pins, needles and sieves for the lead mines, heralding later developments which came on the Derwent with the Industrial Revolution.

Hathersage Leadmill Bridge

Some visitors to Hathersage get little farther than the church gates, or the enclosing railings near its western entrance through which they can see the head and foot stones of the alleged grave of Little John, Robin Hood's hefty henchman. They are unaware that inside the church lies one of the Eyre family who fought at Agincourt, is buried with his wife Joan, and is supported by a representation of their 14 children.

But to view the river, and especially its valley, it is necessary to leave the church and climb up to Millstone Edge, one of the many 'Edges' hereabouts, precipitous grit stone cliffs — commanding an uninterrupted view of the Hope Valley with the Derwent threading its widening way almost from its source; a 'Surprise View' indeed, for those whose approach is from the Edges! Here also are Higgar Tor, a huge outward leaning block on the sky-line believed to be of Celtic origin and Carl Wark, an ancient British fort. This irregular mound of rough mis-shapen stones with enclosures opening into one another, was once presumed to be of the Iron Age but is now considered to belong to the Dark Ages (5th - 6th century). A pause to search for discarded millstones at Lawrencefield to the left of the 'Surprise' is warranted here, if only because the millstone has become a respected indicator of the boundaries of the Peak National Park.

At Grindleford the bridge spanning the Derwent is at the junction of three moorland roads and is one which survived to maintain its position with the advent of the Turnpike roads. They came into being because of the deplorable state of local roads when their upkeep was the responsibility of the parishes. By 1808 there were 1,000 turnpike trusts in England and Wales with over 8,000 toll gates. The style of river crossings changed drastically. Old junctions like Leadmill Bridge at Hathersage declined, and new ones grew with the turnpikes dominated by inns to serve the stagecoaches running between Derby, Nottingham and Manchester.

Despite all the changes, the Derwent moved and moves inexorably on. More Edges are left behind. On the left bank Froggatt is bridged, and Curbar and Baslow Edges and the roads coming south create a loop round the village of Calver to the gaunt six-storey cotton mill where Arkwright's patents held good until 1795.

In 1799 the summer flooding Derwent washed away the bridge and part of the mill. Rebuilt with gritstone 3 feet thick, it was 1804 before production was possible but, by 1830, there were 200 workers with wagons along the turnpikes collecting unprocessed cotton from Manchester and returning with spun yarn.

A new goit, leading the water flow round from the Derwent into a wheel house in front of the mill and a weir at Froggatt Bridge, were said to have produced 160 H.P. from the two wheels each 24ft. in diameter and 17ft. wide. The wheels are gone but the fearsome parallel torrents of the Derwent's power continue endlessly back into the river, obscured by trees, under bridges towards Baslow. On the left is Cliff College, for lay preachers. "Is that where they train climbers?" a youthful voice enquires as we walk along.

Baslow is a township boasting four bridges. The oldest, loftily arched and narrow, has a toll-house with the dimensions of a sizeable dog kennel. A personal, well-remembered crossing by horse-drawn wagonette of this bridge was one of the excitements, shortly after World War One, of a Sunday School Trip along the Derwent Valley to Darley Dale. No one then pointed out the Church or even its clockface, with VICTORIA 1897 replacing the more normal figures, an idea of Dr. Welch of Baslow.

Baslow has a penchant for the number '4'. In addition to bridges, it has four sections or districts, known as Ends. There is Nether End, round the Goose Green where the tributary, Bar Brook, flows pleasantly down past the thatched cottages under a bridge built of very many rounded stones. There is Bridge End, which is self-explanatory, Far End which is a little imprecise as is Over End, unless it be known that 'Over' is Old English for a bank or slope. A right turn, after crossing old or new bridges, leads to the ancient village of Bubnell.

The old bridge over the Derwent is still usable but has been superseded by a Derbyshire County Council Bridge of 1920, flat topped and unexciting but much used by traffic heading for Chatsworth.

Wherever possible, the Great Houses of Derbyshire were established near to its rivers. The Duchess of Devonshire writes, "The usual recipe for a country house is a very big valley, a steep and wooded hill behind, a river in front, encompassed by a large garden and an even larger park."

When defence was a necessary requirement, the river had to be in front and below, as at Haddon Hall, on the River Wye.

For the provision of a water supply and its eventual disposal, a flowing river was a considerable asset. In addition to providing a moat - often not bridged until safer days - a river made the disposal of human waste more tolerable.

Hardwick Hall, for example, lacked a moving stream and despite Bess of Hardwick having installed special close stools, with removable containers for disposal by servants, Girouard reminds us that "until the revolutionary invention of back stairs, in the first half of the 17th. century, gentry walking upstairs could meet their faeces of the night before coming down."

Chatsworth, on the Derwent, is admirably sited, though there were those unable to appreciate its position. "A bright diamond ... set in a vile socket of jet" - was one description, which ignored the abilities of percipient Dukes and the likes of Paxton, Paine and Capability Brown.

Much that has happened at Chatsworth is not directly connected with the Stately Home but is inevitably involved with the Derwent. A water driven corn mill has been moved away from the river where it once worked. Perhaps the only private bridge with Traffic Lights, because of its hump backed narrowness, is historical and possibly unique. Paine, after disapointment at Kedleston near Derby when the young Adam supplanted him, built the lovely bridge over the Derwent at Chatsworth. Thousands of animals including fallow deer graze the park and require water as does the modern garden centre, so it is fortunate that there are other resources which supplement the Derwent.

Chatsworth's Emperor Fountain was constructed in great haste by Paxton after the 6th. Duke met the Czar of Russia at Peterhof in 1843. Its water supply drops 350ft. to the Canal Pond from where the fountain hurls its jet to a height of 276 feet. The Fountain plays frequently, and together with the waters of four man-made lakes arriving by the famous cascade, adds to the resources of the Derwent. Since Paxton opened up East Moor, the supply of water seems endless; what a pity the Czar never came to see his fountain overshadowed.

Leaving Chatsworth Park by the road, now with its chattering cattle grid, towards Beeley there is a reminder at the roadside of a former need for horse troughs. One that sufficed to slake the thirst of horses drawing wagonettes still endlessly pipes out water from the hills above, and the region of Calton, presumably where horses that pulled the wagonettes over the arched Baslow bridge, stopped to quench their considerable thirst. Now as then its stream flows on unceasingly, of little use to the mobile traveller unless he has a leaky radiator.

The car driver passes over Paine's narrow but sturdy bridge, leaving Chatsworth behind. Walkers can climb a stile to the right and pass even nearer to the tree lined Derwent, to Rowsley.

Beeley Bridge, Chatsworth

The mobile traveller drives on to the estate village of Beeley, easily by-passed at a sharp turn right, but worth a halt, for it was, in the main, laid out by Paxton for the sixth Duke. 17th. century buildings there include the Hall and part of the Devonshire Arms - a very good restaurant. Heather covered Beeley Moor, (1,200 ft.) looming to the east, is traditional Hob Goblin country. Steep sided gullies there are known as 'sicks'. Soon temporary exit from the National Park is reached as the Derwent and the Peak Park Boundary veer left, the former under the widened stone bridge at Rowsley.

Rowsley Woods to the left are now a little way from the Derwent. Here a double fringe of almost identical houses and a chapel built for railway workers line the road down to Rowsley, recalling that this was a vital rail centre for collecting thousands of gallons of milk daily for despatch to London - until Beeching had his day. This was younger Rowsley. Great Rowsley mentioned in Domesday is on the other side of the Derwent.

But we are set to follow a somewhat chastened and reformed river almost ready, after its heady younger days, to combine in inventive activity as it moves south to fulfil its destiny.

The 15th. century bridge at Darley carries the Winster road over the Derwent. North of the bridge a massive arch near ravaged and hummocked waste tips, and stone blocks tumbled to half their early height, mark the dead site of Mill Close Mine, the richest lead mine in England. Despite the efforts of the great Cornish engine Jumbo which lifted 7,000,000 gallons of water daily from almost 1,000 feet below the level of the Derwent, its life span was ended when it succumbed to water flooding in the deepest levels at the rate of 5,500 gallons every minute. What kind of a river might the Derwent have been, had it flowed through a less porous terrain, or lacked the retaining capacity of the upstream dams?

Upstream from Darley Bridge, Oaker Hill with some Roman connections is very visible to the left, on the horizon as an approach is made from Matlock to Darley Dale on the A6. There is a tale, made famous by a Wordsworth sonnet, of two sycamore trees planted by two brothers going separate ways to seek their fortunes. One of the trees has gone - the other lives, and the brothers "ne'er again embraced upon earth's wide plain."

It is surprising that the otherwise excellent 0.5. Peak District Leisure Guide informs us that isolated Oaker Hill (634 ft) ... "is crowned by two sycamores." Not so, or the tale loses its point. To confirm that Homer occasionally nods, the Guide goes on to tell us that Joseph Whitworth, whose centenary was celebrated in 1987, was the "inventor of the screw thread." Whitworth certainly was the great standardiser of screw heads and proposed a thread angle of 55 degrees, but was anticipated in its production by American Eli Whitney or possibly George Sorocold, a Derbian by adoption, whom Frank Nixon considers a possibility.

Although an adopted son of Darley Dale, Sir Joseph's generosity to the people was enormous. He donated a hospital, a reading room, swimming baths, a recreation ground and a park, to list but some of his benefactions.

More has been written about Matlock and certainly more that is critical, than any other part of Derbyshire. There are eight Matlocks, excluding the hamlets by the river, mounting the heights, exciting scorn and earning praise.

Matlock Bridge with its four arches, and typical triangular recesses for the safety of pedestrians, was widened on the opposite side to take the increasing traffic up and down the dale. It has long been the nodal point where five roads meet but never a possible fording point due to the ferocity of the Derwent, occasionally flooded and impassable even as recently as 1986, despite the water held captive in the dams in the upper reaches.

In 1853, John Smedley was successfully establishing a hydro here, offering rigorous exercise, immersion and the imbibing of spa waters. A funicular railway ascended Matlock Bank to take the visitor to his hydropathic establishment. His cure included the sale of water and air! Smedley found that more profitable than manufacturing hosiery.

Few who succeeded in the various spurts of achievement that characterised the uneven development of the fortunes of people and places in the Matlocks, could have foreseen that in 1956 the County Council would leave Derby, the County Town, for Matlock, and be established in the former Smedley's Hydro.

It leads to a story which may be apocryphal, that when the Council plumbers were dismantling a range of recessed basins along a corridor, providing a supply of 'SPA WATER' at the Hydro, all pipes led unerringly back to the normal water mains.

Matlock Bath was 'born' around 1698 when thermal waters discovered earlier promoted curative treatments. Hydros, hotels, pump rooms and geological museums followed. The water hereabouts is slightly tepid, about 68 degrees F., 14 degrees lower than at Buxton. It is still utilised in the swimming pool at the New Bath Hotel.

The Royal Petrifying Well became both attractive and lucrative in the valley, as a constant spray left a hardened deposit of lime on such incongruous articles as birds' nests and bowler hats.

High Tor represents one of the most striking examples of rock scenery in Derbyshire, rising to 350 feet above the Derwent. It has attracted artists J.M.W. Turner, Wright of Derby, de Loutherbourg and Sir Francis Chantrey, as well as many local painters.

Poets and writers have sought inspiration from it. A typical 19th. Century writer began, "the Graceful Derwent glides along hidden by the overhanging trees that fling their broad leafy boles over its glittering waters, subduing the dazzling brilliance with their sombre shade; at times, it becomes impetuous, even turbulent, as, wasting its strength in whitened foam, it dashes over the rocky fragments that impede its course, then again, it subsides into a rippling current and carols merrily, like a talkative companion by the side of a wayfarer."

April 21st. 1984 saw a modern lease of life in the Derwent Valley of the Matlocks and the Heights of Abraham - so named because of the similarity to terrain scaled by General Wolfe's troops in 1759.

In 1750 there was a Pleasure Garden here, part afforested, with zig zag paths and flowering shrubs. In 1810 a Show Cavern opened, followed about thirty years later by the Great Masson Cavern and the Prospect Tower, both on the site of a lead mine. Nowadays, the Nestus Mine, with its simulated sounds and electric lights, illuminates the past for visitors.

By 1979, donkeys were no longer used for the ascent. Footpaths were rebuilt, 'a cable car system was conceived', and in 1983, a cable car construction company from Grenoble began working from a rough road over the hill.

A helicopter hauled over a thousand feet of one and a half inch diameter cable, forming a continuous loop for 4 groups of 3 cabins supported by towers. The 360 H.P. engine operates the cars controlled by local men trained by the French firm.

Over 568 metres long with a vertical rise of 169 metres, there is a now tremendous view from the cars of the Derwent with canoes, as well as boats, plying north-south beneath.

Cromford Mill

In George III's reign, a man rode steeply downhill into Cromford. Had he been there before or had failure in Nottingham brought him here?

The man, an itinerant human hair dealer when wigs were fashionable, was to die half a millionaire. He was Richard Arkwright, a Lancastrian.

Cromford's special appeal to Richard Arkwright was twofold; firstly its comparative isolation which provided some degree of security, and secondly, its adequate supply of water lead mining did not want. This cheap source of power from Cromford Sough and Bonsall Brook was stored in ponds to activate wheels on each side of Cromford's first cotton Mill in 1771. A wooden launder (gutter) crossed Mill Lane to supply water to an overshot wheel.

The same source provided for Cromford's second (1776) mill

with its pair of overshot or high breast wheels 15 feet in diameter. The original launder which traversed Mill Lane was replaced by an iron one in 1821 and can still be seen.

Like all mill builders except Strutt, Arkwright used tributaries until he built Masson Mill by which time he had perhaps convinced himself that 'if Strutt could, he could' and this was the only challenge left.

Masson Mill (1783) was to be red-bricked and have two rows of 'Venetian' windows with the lunette windows arranged vertically and 'atop' a cupola with a weather vane. It still stands, with more modern extensions laterally, less artistic windows and a chimney stack added. Now electricity has taken over to replace the added power from steam. It is said the original water power from the Derwent, enhanced by a series of rapids in the gorge, when channelled through various water installations, in addition to any effect that the unusual down-curved weir may have, can supply a third of the power necessary to work the mill. And it is still working!

Danger loomed in any wood-framed mill with candles providing illumination. Hundreds of candles flickered into the darkness of Cromford; working hours were long. Local painters were attracted, notably Wright of Derby. 'Surely, his painting of Richard Arkwright's Cotton Mill with all its windows aglow .....for the night shift must have been almost a first along with de Loutherbourg's painting of Colbrookdale,' writes an unknown commentator. Suffice it to add, Turner was not far behind and his sketch book says much about his artistic pleasures here, and on the Derwent.

Another of Arkwright's local interests in 1788 was the Cromford Canal, where in 1793 local industrialists made the impossible become possible, for in those days, as now, it was no use manufacturing goods without the wherewithal to distribute them.

The Anglican St. Mary's Church, within sight and sound of the

Derwent, built by Arkwright, but not consecrated until after his death, was intended as a family mausoleum. It was opened by Arkwright's son, Richard, for public worship. His father was re-buried here, in a bricked up vault, after having been interred at Matlock because the Church he was building at Cromford was delayed due to a fire and was still incomplete at his death in 1792. The funeral was attended by a great crowd of mourners under High Tor, as it passed along the banks of the Derwent.

He had lived, in the beginning, in Rock House and had planned, as his successes grew, a castle - Willersley Castle - above the sight and sound of the Derwent, and looking down on the mill and Cromford, which were both of his making.

Both Arkwright at Cromford and Jedediah Strutt at Belper further down stream were pioneers and well ahead of their times, not only in industrial expertise but in concern for their workers. They introduced and developed the factory system with a degree of humanity not very prevalent in those days, and provided reasonable accommodation for their workers. Even though mothers and children were working relatively long hours, John Farey could write in his General View of the County, 'The cottagers are much better provided with habitation than ... in the Southern Counties.'

By 1777, Arkwright had built homes and a school in North Street, Cromford, named not according to the compass, but in honour of the Prime Minister, Lord North.

In 1924 these houses passed out of the hands of the Arkwright family but Derbyshire County Council, rightly, refused to sanction their destruction. Now in the ownership of trustees their historical survival is assured. The school still functions.

After early development in Derby, Jedediah Strutt and Richard Arkwright of Cromford, were beginning a considerable partnership. In 1770, Strutt had two mills in Derby, one at Markeaton Brook and another at Gaol Brook, both tributaries of the Derwent, though now both culverted. Silk had opened up industry on the Derwent, but difficulties in getting silk created problems and the cotton industry overtook and supplanted it.

The enterprising partnership and their adoption of the factory system produced a string of successful waterpowered cotton mills in Derbyshire, then Staffordshire, Lancashire, Yorkshire and Scotland - based on the established traditions of Derbyshire. In 1816, Jedediah's son, William, was telling a Select Committee that children were working 12 hours a day - 6 before and 6 after dinner, allowing time for breakfast and tea - an invariable practice for a century.

At Belper, and in their Derby early timber-framed mills, the Strutts were well aware of the threat of fire.

Oil, wood, grease and cotton dust could combine and produce flash-fires, causing total destruction with frightening rapidity. Illumination by candles as mentioned earlier was a constant hazard.

Jedediah's eldest son, William, always called Billy by his father, lived at St. Helen's House, Derby. He now looks out benignly from his portrait by Reinagle in the entrance hall, on the many adult students who use his former family home for their adult educational activities.

It was Billy who tackled the problem of fire. His earlier knowledge of metals led him to encase the wooden framework - always at risk initially. Later, metal stanchions followed on brick or tiled floors. Arches of brick were constructed. Weight reduction became necessary on top floors and pots were constructed to make hollow-ware arches. West Hallam Pottery made these 'pots.' The bottle kiln there is still in operative existence concentrating on artistic output rather than on mill fire precautions. In 1803, Jedediah's North Mill at Belper was rebuilt, iron-framed throughout, by William after what the Derby Mercury described as 'a most tremendous fire!'

The need for paper in the early 18th. Century caused merchants who had to purchase abroad, to seek supplies in England. By 1700 there were paper mills on the Derwent at Duffield, Darley Abbey and Masson. Richard Arkwright became involved in 1768 - 1772, but the largest mill, the Peckwash near Little Eaton, was built by Thomas Tempest in 1805. He had a charter of 1425 renewed with the right to take up to 800 H.P. from the Derwent.

He erected extensive buildings on the river below Duffield Bridge, where by 1850 there were five large waterwheels operating the biggest paper mill in England, and some say, in Europe.

About 1894 two steam turbines were installed. The very visible chimney built at the same time stands as a memento to a Mr. Catt who lived on the hill adjoining the mill. An injunction awarded to him restrained the mill from emitting smoke which the prevailing wind carried to cause a nuisance.

Since 1906 the chimney has not smoked, and in fact the present owner of the site told the writer that he had never been able to find the flue leading to the offending chimney!

Now only overgrown remains of the mill buildings, leats, pools and channels lie in disorder as the Derwent flows by.

Having squeezed through the Chevin, the hilly centre of Duffield Frith, important in Norman times with its castle on its right bank, and Hopping Hill on its left, with rows of Strutt's workers' stone cottages, the Derwent faces a more placid descent through an increasingly pastoral scene. Apart from the former coal wharf at Little Eaton and the now closed mill replacing Peckwash, Allestree where the Evans family lived, is one of Derby's pleasanter suburbs.

The Evans family, like those of Arkwright and Strutt, were caring mill-owners living in the community. Their home was in Allestree Park with its lake and now a communal golf course. Allestree Hall (1795) has an uncertain future.

Ford Lane which leads from Matlock Road (A6) to the A38

Trunk Road indicates a former river crossing at river level. From there the Derwent flows on under modern bridges to Darley Abbey.

Parts of the ancient Abbey mingle with the remains of old factory workers' houses and the cotton mill where the toll bridge over the Derwent was recently re-opened.

Former mill buildings house small industries and 'one man' businesses. The Darley workers' cottages are much in demand and a lively community has grown up to maintain village life.

On the eastern bank of the Derwent, the Evans' mill erected in 1783 was powered 'through a wheelhouse by a diagonal weir 6ft. high and 360 ft. long only to be destroyed by fire 5 years later.' Jedediah Strutt's early uninsured North Mill at Belper was destroyed by fire in 1803, in spite of the fact that he had nailed thousands of foot-square tin sheets on the wooden beams the best precautions then contrived against fire.

Thomas Evans, after his father's death in 1746, acquired in

The Boar's Head Mill, Derby

1783, lead mines at Bonsall, slitting mills at the Holms on the Derwent in Derby, then built with sons Walter and William the Boar's Head Mill, named after the crest on his family's coat-of-arms.

He also established a bank in Derby in 1771. Arkwright was one of his early customers and persuaded Thomas, then 60 years old, to build and operate the mill, under licence from him. During the building, Arkwright was a partner and it seems likely that 'Billy' Strutt and also his sister Elizabeth may have had shares. But it was certainly his alone, when Thomas Evans died in 1814 worth £800,000.

Further downstream, the Derwent has given up some of its secrets of the Roman occupation at Little Chester, the Roman fort of Derventio, dated about AD 55-60 in the reign of Emperor Nero. At Strutt's Park vestiges of bridge foundations still attract attention, and further south, near the racecourse and Sports Ground, limited excavations have revealed a Roman burial area with funeral ornaments.

Three years before Bonny Prince Charlie made his abortive visit to Derby, Daniel Defoe was touring Britain and noting 'a curiosity of a very extraordinary nature... I mean those mills on the Derwent ... the only ones in England ... making Organzine or Thrown Silk ... 318,504,960 yards (in 24 hrs.) .. time the Water-wheel goes round.'

Thomas Cotchett, born in Mickleover in 1640, was trained as a barrister at Gray's Inn, London. He became a silk reeler when Italian refugees fled from Louis XIV of France, to where the Huguenots had settled in Spitalfields' wool weaving centre. At that time silk thread had to be imported from Italy where it was spun on water powered machines. Cotchett realised he could make a fortune if he could introduce machines to power silk weaving in England.

In 1702 he built a three storied silk mill on the By Flatt, an island on the Derwent near the Fulling Mills hence the nearby 'Full

Street.' Pevsner confirms that this was the site of the first mill in England.

Cotchett was fortunate to secure the services of George Sorocold to instal Dutch spinning machines driven by a 13½ ft. diameter water wheel.

Sorocold was actually an academic who married a Derby girl and settled in the town in 1684. He had rehung the bells of All Saints, now Derby Cathedral, and installed the first local water supply from the Derwent, carried along in bored elm tree trunks to a supply tank in St. Michael's Churchyard, for local distribution to those subscribing to his scheme which worked for 150 years. Sorocold's fame as a water engineer quickly spread as far as London.

He was again engaged as the engineer when Thomas and John Lombe's much larger, five storied mill superseded Cotchett's mill 15 or 16 years later.

Sir Thomas Lombe, a wealthy silk merchant of Norwich and London, had his younger half brother apprenticed to Cotchett and it was he who sent John to Italy, either on a genuine visit or a mission of industrial espionage, which resulted in the success of the silk industry so early in Derby. Sorocold had the task of making and fitting toothed wheels and bobbins in thousands for spinning reels, twist and winding bobbins, spindles and hundreds of star wheels. 94,206 moving parts motivated from a single source of water power.

He was particularly fortunate to be able to play his considerable part in the success of the mill, for the paddles of the water wheel he designed to operate the Italian machines caught him up and took him into the Derwent. Fortunately the same paddle that took him under water threw him back on dry land. ... A reciprocal favour?

The old silk mill is now the Derby Industrial Museum.

The apprentices in the Silk Mill were the least appreciative of its activities. One wrote that his seven years were the most miserable of his life and it was his great misfortune to be born in Derby. But both owner and apprentices' parents welcomed the income. Soon there were not enough apprentices available and masters sought replacements from the Poor Houses in what has been described as 'its most pernicious phase.'

Few of the owners provided conditions as good as Arkwright and the Strutts. Long hours and harsh discipline were common and the worst conditions were often imposed by overseers who had earlier been apprentices. Nevertheless the millowners on the Derwent, Arkwright at Cromford and the Strutts at Milford and Belper generally set standards on which subsequent enlightened factory regulations were based.

After its considerable contribution to industrial history in Derby, the Derwent flows on ignoring a claim in the 1977 Derbyshire Guide, that 'the great works of the Midland Railway provided Derby's only significant claim to industrial importance.'

The Silk Mill

A contrary opinion is expressed by Brian Cooper in his book, "The Transformation of a Valley - the Derbyshire Derwent":-

"Standing by the Silk Mill in Derby, it is difficult to escape the feeling, that here on this narrow strip of land by the Derwent, a vital part of our modern world was born, the achievement of - Thomas Lombe, mercer, John Lombe, silk mechanic, George Sorocold, engineer."

It is remarkable that Derby should have been in at the beginning of textile fabrication, with three basic important fibres:- wool, with the development of additions to the Knitting Frame by Jedediah Strutt to create the Derby Rib; silk, the work of the pioneers indicated above, with the thread from the silkworm cocoon; and artificial silk, created chemically. All produced on the banks of the Derwent and drawing on its water supplies.

The early shape of the Derwent immediately south of the old St. Mary's Bridge is most difficult to envisage. Buildings, road works and realignments have obscured outlines of the river that formerly left its configuration much like the traditional sketch of a ham bone. As it moved under the former Derwent Bridge, it broadened into the first bulge; now it has to negotiate the modern Causey Bridge from which a former island, shaped like an elongated penknife, seems to have shrunk from the land. The knuckle of the bone has shrunk too, towards the By Flatt Island.

A wedge of land widens out as the Derwent leaves Derby to the south-east, with railway installations and gas works, then a singularly empty wedge until Raynesway is reached.

After passing under road and rail bridges, the Derwent contorts into three meanders alongside Nottingham Road, which is very straight as befits its early alignment by the Romans. The first of these loops holds within it the Sewage Works and the Waste Disposal Plant.

Also relying on the Derwent are the filter bed and sludge

lagoons and growing nearby in season, a profusion of tomato plants from a once-consumed but apparently indestructible seed.

The next loop downstream was constructed towards the end of the 1914-18 war in the early years of British Celanese, now Courtauld's Acetate. The parent company was formed by Huguenot, George Courtauld at Braintree, Essex. At Spondon, the purpose was to discover a nonflammable paint for aircraft.

Within this river loop are two lakes, West and East, created when aggregate was dug out to facilitate the building of the early factory in the 1920's and to allow silt to settle before water was used on site for production and cooling purposes.

This area, apart from its functional supply of treated Derwent water, has become a considerable nature reserve with paths of chip wood through groves of seedpopping balsam and great trees, to wooden 'hides' on the edge of each lake for an uninterrupted view of water birds, which have an excellent habitat here.

Viewing is by invitation only but open days are arranged from time to time. Some of the birds which were seen on the writer's visit were grebe, teal, pochard, wigeon, mallard, dabchick, kingfisher, coot and tufted duck.

As the lakes are never frozen, their relatively warm water attracts birds in winter when there are as many as 7 - 800 visitors with a variety of fish populating the river, lakes and clear water factory drains.

The nature reserve is living proof of the effective purification of the water passed on eventually to the Trent - and later into the North Sea.

The Derwent water is filtered, cleaned and circulated by massive pumps. Water contaminated by chemicals is directed to the Severn Trent Water Board for cleaning before being returned to the Derwent. 45 million gallons of water are normally used daily but the plant has a capacity for dealing with 90 million gallons.

The third loop is a multiple meander. After passing the former Spondon Power Station now used to produce steam for Courtauld, a mill race to the north is named The Stryne. This is an old name for a stream or watercourse, also found in North Derbyshire in the Goyt Valley 'visited' later. A double stream takes the water under the bridge at Station Road, Borrowash, where it becomes one stream enclosing Little Stryne.

Not far from the river, on the Nottingham Road, as it leaves Borrowash, there is recent housing development named Barrons' Way, after William Barron, a Scot, head gardener at nearby Elvaston Castle and a great aboriculturalist. He evolved a method of transplanting mature trees from one area to another to enable the Earl of Harrington to have a variety of forest trees maturing in his life-time. On retirement, Barron started market gardening in Borrowash.

The Derwent is now nearing the end of its journey, tapering out 50 miles from the sea at Wilne. Wilne in great variety; Great, Little, South Ferry and Church. It is easier to seek Shardlow than Wilne and more rewarding.

Anyone seriously wishing to visit Shardlow needs Arkwright Society's guide No. 18, Canal-Shardlow. Willden Ferry is Shardlow. It is possible to drive through this old inland port and see disappointingly little. The A6 is not very revealing. But to left and to right and at the site of the old washed-away Cavendish Bridge is the story of an inland port that came with the era of canal construction and was only equalled by Stourport.

James Brindley, born in Derbyshire, superb mental calculator, never known to use pencil or paper, attracted attention by building a canal for the Duke of Bridgewater, to carry coal from his Worsley Colliery to Manchester. He had overcome the obstacle of the River Irwell by putting an aqueduct over it. Four great esturial ports - London, Bristol, Liverpool and Hull were proposed to cut out long sea voyages. In 1765, alternative proposals were afoot, both beginning at Willden Ferry; the first was to go via the Weaver to the

29

Mersey at Runcorn, the second to Preston Brook, linking Manchester to the Mersey at Runcorn.

Wedgwood and Erasmus Darwin supported the second, the Grand Trunk Canal, later renamed Trent and Mersey.

Brindley was to construct the canal to go south-west from Derwent Mouth to Trent, near Shardlow, but he died unexpectedly, following a severe chill caused by a heavy wetting in a violent storm, during which he refused to stop working. His brother-in-law, Henshall, completed the canal from the Trent to Preston Brook via Burton, Rugeley and Stoke Middlewich. Hence the sign on the canal bank at Shardlow: Preston Brook 92 miles.

Population had quadrupled from 1789 - 1841 and development on the canal and its banks produced the still to be seen, left and right of the main road, canals, old locks and taverns. Cafes, restaurants and modern marinas followed. Warehouses have been refitted for corn milling and storage. Some narrow boats have been converted for week-end recreation and holidays afloat. Recreational boat building flourishes.

There is an interesting rope-walk for an exchange of normal canal short ropes for the long needed when towing on the Trent. The old Clock Warehouse of 1780 has a neat arch at water level to take boats which needed to unload without wetting their cargo. It is now a museum of canal memorabilia and a restaurant.

Forsake the main road and veer to left or right inquisitively. On to Paine's Bridge, washed away in modern times and replaced temporarily by a Bailey Bridge until the new bridge could be erected, straight as a die, and on to the M1. The old toll board adds interest to the scene.

At times there really does seem to have been two Derwents but at Great Wilne there are indications that soon there will be but one. As W.H. Brighouse explains 'finally the Derwent makes a last

The Old Clock Warehouse, Shardlow

double bend into the open and, at Derwent Mouth, comes into head-on collision with the Trent.'

As the Soar from Leicestershire also joins in, it is a very long way from the little 'Clapper Bridges' of the north, those rough hewn gritstone slabs, to the modern motorway bridge hereabouts spanning the augmented Trent on its thick sloping supports near water-level.

OTHER RIVERS AND STREAMS

Though road, rail and canal became interconnected and their developers joined in many enterprises and evolving industries which combined, the rivers must continue to be our main concern. The Derwent, full of character, dominates as it flows on, absorbing waters that no less attractively promote its flow.

In his summary of Derbyshire rivers, John Leyland forgets 'the gentle Etheroe' which makes its way to the Mersey, but not the Alport, Sett and Shoo rivers, the Dunsley Spring, the Kinder Downfall and a rich assortment of brooks, including Ladybower and Ladygate, Bonsall, Henmore, Hood, Hurst, Mill, Little Howden, Red and Nun's Shelf, Tideswell and Warm.

The few tributaries entering on the left bank of the Derwent are the Alport, Ashop and Kinder making minor contributions as well as Abbey Brook, the Amber and the Erewash.

Entering by the right bank are the Ashop, Noe, Peakshole Water, the Wye, Lathkill and Bradford, Bonsall Brook, the Ecclesbourne and Markeaton Brook.

The Noe

Rivers have names which have probably been in use for two thousand years. The 'Noe' simply means to flow. Burdetts map of Derbyshire of 1791 spells it 'Now'.

Joined from the north by three brooks of note, Ollerbrook, Ladybooth Brook and a brook from Jaggers Clough, its source being at Edale near the southern end of the Pennine Way, going north along Grindsbrook.

In Buxton Museum there is a Roman milestone from the Roman road which follows Batham Gate (the Road to the Baths) which once linked Navio, the fort at Brough, on the River Noe.

32

Peaksholewater

Peaksholewater submerges in Peak Cavern, hence its name.

On the floor of the entrance, artifically and expensively blasted open in search of lead. In the 18th. Century, rope makers plied a trade four hundred years old. Within living memory, orders for 8 miles of string were undertaken and the family tradition maintained of presenting each local bride with a clothes line. The smoke-stained ceiling shows where cottages existed near the rope walk, still in situ, with the eternal stream continually flowing out alongside.

Many visitors take guided tours of the Cavern during the summer and the writer recalls taking in a party of Norwegian teachers. At one point in the tour, the guide held aloft a bucket into which a drop of water fell from the cave roof with an audible 'plop'. He then invited any of the party to take the bucket and catch a drop. Several visitors accepted the invitation, carefully standing on the exact spot chosed by the guide, but without success.

The guide again took the bucket and held it nonchalantly aloft. "Lerrit come, Joe", he commanded, and instantly, a drop hit the bottom of the bucket.

The Wye

The Wye, as John Leyland reminds us after his visit in 1891, "flows in a south easterly direction from the hills above Buxton through Ashwood, Chee, Miller's Dale and Monsall Dale to Ashford and Bakewell ... receives the waters of the Lathkill and falls into the Derwent at Rowsley."

The River Wye is said to be formed by three springs, 'I, Thou and He united plurally to We'. It is agreed to be one of the prettiest of Derbyshire rivers, and perhaps one of the best known because of the limestone uplands and superb dales, and on account of Buxton and Bakewell, not to mention Haddon Hall, all of which are good reasons for visitors to become aware of the river.

Yet Buxton, probably more concerned with boosting the curative properties of its local 'spa' waters has failed to make the Wye an attractive, visible asset.

Anyone fortunate enough to have visited Annecy in the French Haute-Savoie, will have seen how Buxton could have been made attractive by allowing the River Wye to have continued its course through the town, instead of being obscured beneath heavy gritstone buildings.

Downstream the Wye passes a scene of early injustice to pauper children at Litton Mill. With Cressbrook Mill a mile further down stream, early cotton industry flourished here till halted by fire. In 1810 William Newton was back to rebuild, damn the Wye, and hew away the rock to recreate, in 1815, the mill as still seen today, with the lovely Water-cum Joly, an attractive pool to power two large waterwheels.

Haddon Hall

Monsall Dale is not far away, irrevocably connected with Ruskin. He fulminated about the railway, not because he resisted progress, but because another route was ignored on the ground of expense, which would not have violated a lovely river valley. Now trees almost obscure the Viaduct and its lost railway from the vantage point where most people park their cars to enjoy the lovely dale ahead.

Young trout were raised for anglers fishing expensively lower down the stream at Ashford-in-the-Water -and one expects it often was fished - before man extracted so much water to power early mills for polishing 'marble' found near at hand in Rookery Mine. Henry Watson, of Bakewell, polished it from dull grey to black as seen at Chatsworth House and Hardwick Hall embellishing ducal fireplaces, and now threatening a return to the original grey of the millions of years old crinoids.

The Wye here attracts artists, especially with its "Sheepwash Bridge", with vented curling gritstone ends, to prevent fearful sheep from crowding to the point of suffocation. Sheepwashing now is a luxury reserved for visitors during Welldressings.

The Wye now has a modern bridge crossing the Buxton to Bakewell road into the village. White Watson had a water powered mill here to cut slices of rock for mounting to illustrate geology.

The Church has some black marble and also 'virgin crants', Shakespeare's 'crantses', paper garlands carried on coffins of maidens and hung in church later.

As usual with dale streams, the Wye, Dove and Lathkill are noted for their fishing. An unusual sight in the past was Dora Oliver, a female water bailiff, on the Hartington stretch of the Dove, out in mid-stream giving a party of school children a very practical lesson on river ecology and its protection.

These rivers are stocked with trout for syndicates, hotel chains and the like and those who pay for fly fishing. Walt. Unsworth relates that in 1970, 2,700 rainbow trout and 1,000 brown trout were added to the Wye, though he adds, "I have never seen anyone fishing in the river. Perhaps I go at the wrong time." Certainly he was not about when John Julius Norwich caught his first rainbow trout at the Dorothy Vernon 'escape bridge' at Haddon!

The bridge over the Wye at Bakewell dated about 1300, has triangular quoins, five Gothic arches and is a splendid specimen of its kind. Holme Bridge, a narrow bridge further upstream, over 350 years older, was erected to give an approach to Holme Hall.

Arkwright promoted increased trade with Bakewell with the discovery of Derbyshire chert. This replaced 'boulders' to grind flint to powder to mix with clay and produce a whiter body, free from black spots. Packhorses carried two bags each of one hundredweight before first the canals and then the railway transported it to the Potteries. Galena, a sulphide of lead, was also transported from Holme Bank Quarry to the Potteries to give an improved glaze.

Lathkill and Bradford

The Wye has almost run its pleasant course; it has yet to receive the Lathkill and Bradford.

The Lathkill rises in winter in a cave, south east of Monyash. In dry spells, the river rises near Over Haddon and often it is necessary to rescue fish from the river's dry upper reaches. Between Monyash and the delightful little hamlet of Alport, where long pack horse trains branched off over the moors, the course of the Lathkill is a beautiful valley, with a clear tumbling river, woodland and spectacular limestone buttressed sides. The Lathkill, alone among Derbyshire rivers, completes its course almost entirely in limestone country. Charles Cotton, using a more consistent plural than currently employed and, apparently, quoting an unspecified source, puts in a good word for the Lathkill.

"It is the most transparent stream I ever saw and breeds, 'tis said, the reddest Trouts in England."

36

Brian Cooper, in his excellent book 'The Transformation of a Valley', writes, "Of all the mining fields, none is more evocative than Lathkill Dale, of desperate struggles (of the miners) against underground waters, from the 13th. century onwards, especially in the Mandale Mines." Present tranquillity here and in the Bradford Dale makes this unbelievable, apart from evident signs of waterwheels, soughs and engine houses.

It is tempting to be torn away from the rivers and to tell of the struggle to fight waters that did not conform to pattern but sank deep into the limestone. This pattern that amounts almost to waywardness is characteristic of both the Lathkill and the Bradford. They disappear - leaving the river bed dry. The reverse process follows in wetter periods, at points known as 'swallets' where pressure is relieved by water that surfaces, notably at Cales Dale, where there is a Lathkill Nature Reserve.

Lathkill Dale

Large clear pools mark the Bradford, two miles from its 'source' when there is no surface water. But at Dale Farm underlying rocks allow a flow into the Lathkill, and jointly they then flow into the Wye fresh from Haddon, and under Fillyford Bridge, serving the village of Congreave, to re-activate the flour mill at Rowsley before joining the Derwent, by the two-arched little bridge.

The Dove

The Dove, which rises on the slopes of Axe Edge, becomes, until it reaches the Trent, the Derbyshire Staffordshire county boundary.

Underlying rocks determine its scenery. The gritstone at source may have little effect, except for a rugged grandeur, but the limestone certainly has. A rainfall of 50 inches annually is carried away, some subterraneously, from Axe Edge near the A53 Buxton-Leek Road, where snow often lingers till spring. Here is the watershed giving rise to five important rivers; the Dove, Manifold, the Wye, the Goyt and the Dane.

The first two are soon in the White Peak - so called because of the colour of the outcropping rocks which is actually light grey. Rain water and streams, penetrate this rock in swallets to form underground streams - a strange underground, wet world, where curious channels can be formed, leading in places, to 'lost rivers' and in others to 'lush dales'. Some of these dales are only for walkers and anglers.

This is the world immortalised by Isaac Walton. 'The Incomparable Dove' he called it and he and his friend Cotton spent hours here which ought to have been spent more gainfully elsewhere, hence the need for a 'bolt-hole' in a Wolfscote Dale cave where he could escape his creditors!

The Dove skirts Buxton and, despite the commonly known name for this part of Derbyshire, peaks are rare, and shapely hills guard the entrance to Dovedale. Tight loops of the Dove have made cuttings into the limestone. Parson Gilpin was 'greatly surprised'. He found the Dale 'chaste, picturesque and beautiful to a high degree.'

In Dovedale, impermeable rocks have left such features as Tissington Spires, Lover's Leap and part of early caverns formed by relentless water power. The famous ashwoods are unlikely to be natural. Ring counting shows their age to be, at most, 200 years. They were probably planted to control ever spreading heather, a common procedure to improve fertility.

The early desolation from Axe Edge to Ashbourne caused landowners to move the population south to more productive areas around Ashbourne. The Manifold, having captured nothing bigger than the Tean, now joins the Dove at Ilam, which is completely in Staffordshire, but has for many visitors become part of Dovedale. Dovedale has not lacked those who sing its praises. It has been said that "in spite of its peerless beauty it is the most modest of rivers, hiding itself; where it is at its best ... it lurks unseen, no highway quite reaches it ... it can only be seen by walking."

The Dove now continues its way to the west of the thousand feet high Thorpe Cloud which gives or takes its name from the village hidden off the main road to Ashbourne. The village church has a Norman Tower built in the days of King Stephen.

Henmore Brook

It is the Henmore Brook that provides the damp environment for old scores to be settled between 'uppards and downards' in Ashbourne Street Football on Shrove Tuesday with a repeat performance the following day. Ashbourne, the market town, attracts visitors now as it has done for centuries, and probably is less in need of publicity than any market town north of the Trent.

After the confluence of Dove and Trent at the ancient home of the Norman de Solneys, there were difficulties of even minor navigation, for a sandbank formed a barrier to 18th. century

39

Entrance to Dovedale

commerce, presumably barrels of Burton beer. But this gave a new
lease of life to Willington higher up the river where an inland port
developed, prior to the opening of the Trent Mersey Canal.

The Trent is normally considered to be a Nottinghamshire
River but it plays its part in the history of Southern Derbyshire and
also Staffordshire. Paleolithic period stone axes have been found in
the Derbyshire Trent gravel. The Danes were wintering at Repton in
871-2, and the river then was much nearer to what is now Repton
College. Today it is bridged nearer Willington. In 1523 grain came
into Derbyshire via Hull and the Trent. Swarkeston Bridge was the
last winter crossing from south to north and many aggressors were
stopped there by its marshy approach before the river was reached.

The Amber

The River Amber, almost the only tributary of consequence

coming in on the left bank of the Derwent from the "broad and prosperous" area around Ashover, with crags such as Cocking Tor seen above Overton Hall, one time home of Sir Joseph Banks, a naturalist with Cook on his Round World Voyage. In the winter of 1788 a meeting attended by Arkwright at Matlock was invited "to support a Navigation (Canal) from Derby to Cromford and up the River Amber."

The Amber, between its source and eventual arrival at the Derwent in Ambergate, feeds Ogston Reservoir, popular with the angling fraternity and inland sailors.

The Goyt

The Goyt is the one Derbyshire river which leaves the County in a northerly direction. Rising on Axe Edge near the well-known landmark, the Cat and Fiddle Inn, it veers northerly to Whaley Bridge, and meanders northwesterly via New Mills to Marple, looping more generally westerly to Stockport. Finally it ceases to be a Derbyshire river, joins the Tame to form the Mersey and to flow into the Irish Sea.

Its course, an obvious water gathering area, was used first in 1938 for the Fernilee Reservoir, holding just over a million gallons, and then the Errwood Reservoir completed in 1967, holding 927,000 gallons and costing one and a half million pounds more. Both were built by the then Stockport and District Water Board.

Because of the proximity of Buxton, Stockport, Marple, New Mills and Macclesfield, developments have taken place in the Valley to provide recreational activities. Waymarked walks, car parks and picnic areas are indicated as part of a scheme initiated, in 1970-71, by the Countryside Commission and the Peak Park Planning Board, following traffic experiments. The co-operation of the North West Water Authority, as landowners, and the Forestry Commission has enabled maintenance of reasonable access and movement, following experimental 'park and ride' arrangements.

During the last half century, a thriving farming community has met with considerable change. The Grimshawes built Errwood Hall in 1830 - lasting for 100 years before the Fernilee Reservior was built. It had its own school, water-mill, cemetery and even a coal mine, and the Dale O'Goyte sheep, a speckled faced Derbyshire Gritstone, was the 'back bone' of the 30 farms. The hamlet of Goyt's Bridge 'perished' in the flooding, but the old pack horse bridge, used for smuggling salt from Cheshire during the incidence of the salt tax, was re-erected upstream, near Goytsclough Quarry, a picnic area. This quarry was the base for Pickfords, who first settled for mineral extraction and haulage before their move into national removal and, more recently, travel.

A further mile beyond is the traffic-free wooded clough site of Errwood Hall where rhododendrons in June are a pleasant reminder of the Grimshawes who first planted them. Further south is Derbyshire Bridge - now a reminder that a boundary was moved in 1928 putting the river further into Cheshire. Further north, the Street, a Roman Road to Pym Chair, offers a ridge walk with extensive views.

The Drone

The routes that opened up the Rother, Doe Lea and Erewash Valleys, led eventually to the need for the Chesterfield-Sheffield route away from the narrow valleys, and the use of yet another Derbyshire river valley, that of the Drone, which gave its name to Dronfield.

Burdett's Map of Derbyshire of 1791 shows clearly the Drone flowing through Dronfield, Unstone and Shepherd's Bridge - now Sheepbridge, but omitting all but one of the six water mills then operating in Dronfield. Industry here produced edge tools, "with all its stir of spades and shovels, tools for the workshop and sickles for the field", as described in 'The King's England'. It omits the workshop that lasted longest with the introduction of the tilt hammer, and known to all as the 'Tilt' which proclaimed the hours of the working day with its far-reaching hooter!

The Goyt

A little further along the main road, high on the left bank was the Grammar School of Henry Fanshawe (1506-68) Remembrancer of the Exchequer to Queen Elizabeth, who by his will dated 1567, endowed the school where the writer spent happy and fruitful days long past.

The Rother Valley

The North Midland Railway Company opened its line between Derby and Rotherham on 11th. May 1840, choosing to follow the Valley of the River Rother from Chesterfield via Staveley and Beighton. During 1863, 100,000 tons of coal and 40,000 tons of pig iron from one firm, used this line from Clay Cross and S.E. Derbyshire. Interested parties brought congestion to Sheffield in December 1863 and again in 1864. It was that industrial development that caused a certain 19th. century squalor to arise.

After joining the Don in South Yorkshire the Rother heads towards the sea.

Roy Christian describes the rivers here as 'inconsequential' and the area one 'on which industry had laid heavy hands'. Some of the less responsible commentators find it easy, but none the less offensive, to refer constantly to the "Dirty Rother." Whilst it may be true that some of the squalor comes from coal and iron, there are those who say things are not so bad as they are painted.

The Managing Director of Staveley Chemicals pointed out that in the Clean Rivers Campaign, his company is in an area where the river, currently listed as grade four on a pollution scale of one to four, was much less polluted than had been suggested. He claimed moorhens, kingfishers and other riverside creatures were regularly to be seen, whilst water plants and sticklebacks were to be found in a tributary flowing through the works complex. "We are spending a great deal of money to solve our effluent problems", he said.

Envoi

A re-reading of 'The Unknown Island' by S.P.B. Mais, a Devonian by birth, but proudly of Derbyshire by adoption as the son of a Derbyshire vicar, reminds one of how relatively recently has the freedom to go unhampered, for instance, to the sources of Derbyshire rivers, been achieved. His complaints were that his journeyings were spoiled by having to keep to the path. "There are no paths on Dartmoor", he protests.

It leads him to say, "The sooner Kinder Scout ceases to be a grouse moor and becomes a National Park the better." This plea comes from a book first published in 1932.

S.P.B. Mais would surely have been delighted to know that the Peak District he knew so well became a National Park on 17th. April 1951, opening the exciting way for those that followed.

Would he have been so delighted to know that the proposal to

44

set up, in 1989, a National Rivers Authority, may threaten a return of pre 1951 closures of land and amenities drained by the Derbyshire Rivers? A forbidding 40th anniversary.

SHEEPWASH BRIDGE — ASHFORD-IN-THE WATER

Sheep now are only washed on high days and holidays. The double wall enclosure has missing stones for ventilation for crowding of fearful sheep. *Photo by Harold W. Fearnehough*

BIBLIOGRAPHY

Derbyshire	Roy Christian	1978
The Peak District	Roy Christian	1976
The Transformation of a Valley	Brian Cooper	1983
Portrait of the River Derwent	Walt Unsworth	1971
Birchinlee	Brian Robinson	1983
0.S. Leisure Guide -Peak District		1987
The Derbyshire Wye and Lathkill Dale	Brian Spencer and John Robey	1973
Matlock and Upper Derwent Valley	Brian Spencer and John Robey	1975
Water Under the Bridge – a Short History of the Dams	V.J. Hallam	1979
The Illustrated History of Derbyshire	John Heath	1982
History of Derbyshire William Wooley	Glover & Riden	1981
Bulmer's Derby - 1895	D.C.C. Reprint	1988
Peakland Roads and Trackways	A.E. Dodd E.M. Dodd	1974
First and Last	Peak Park Planning Board	1978
Derbyshire Life and Countryside	Many issues	
Derby - an Illustrated History	Maxwell Craven	1988
The Rivers and Streams of England	A.G. Bradley	1985

46

ABOUT THE AUTHOR

Apart from a period spent in training for the teaching profession, the author has spent the whole of his life in Derbyshire. Born in the north-east of the County at Dronfield Woodhouse, near Sheffield, then with only a hundred houses. He has also lived in Chesterfield, Sudbury, Mosbrough and finally Derby, with headships in the last three places.

His wife also has held headships in Derbyshire, as has their son and daughter-in-law. Their daughter is also a teacher. The author has retired twice, most recently from the travel industry which allowed him to travel abroad extensively. For the last ten years he has been showing groups of people some of the delights of Derbyshire. He writes a little and looks out over the Chevin.

ACKNOWLEDGEMENTS

The author gratefully acknowledges the assistance of the Severn Trent Water Authority for verbal and written help. Dr. Brian Robinson of Manchester University who wrote 'Birchinlee' and told me the history of a lady who was most kind to me when I was a young choir-boy. Mrs. Arthur Farnsworth, wife of the organist of Dore Church was also the widow of Mr. Trippett of Birchinlee, which I never knew till I read Dr. Robinson's book.

Also much appreciated was the help of Courtauld's Acetate, on my visit to their 25 acre Nature Reserve and the especially helpful information of Mr. Trevor Fox. As always, gratitude must be expressed to the ladies of my local Allestree Library and the Derby Local Studies Library.

Finally, to my wife Evelyn, unfailingly helpful, who now functions most efficiently as my memory.

THE DERWENT AT DARLEY ABBEY

The Evans family water-powered late 18th century cotton mills flourished here. The buildings still work in small industrial units but the Derwent only pleases the eye and gives way to electric power.   *Photo by Harold W. Fearnehough*

The illustrations in this book were produced by a second year student at Derbyshire College of Higher Education, Caroline Abrahams, as part of a six week work experience. The undertaking and successful completion of such projects by all students is regarded by the college as a vital component of their BA (Hons) degree, aiming to provide students with practical and necessary experience of a working environment outside of study with the belief that this will be beneficial to the education they have received.